Artists at Work
Wood Artists

Cheryl Jakab

MACMILLAN
LIBRARY

First published in 2006 by
MACMILLAN EDUCATION AUSTRALIA PTY LTD
627 Chapel Street, South Yarra 3141

Visit our website at www.macmillan.com.au

Associated companies and representatives throughout the world.

National Library of Australia
Cataloguing-in-Publication data

Jakab, Cheryl.
    Wood artists.

    Includes index.
    For upper primary school aged children.
    ISBN 978 0 7329 9863 9.
    ISBN 0 7329 9863 8.

    1. Woodwork – Juvenile literature. I. Title. (Series:
    Jakab, Cheryl. Artists at work).

736.4

Edited by Sam Munday
Text and cover design by Karen Young
Page layout by Karen Young
Photo research by Jes Senbergs
Illustrations by Ann Likhovetsky

Printed in China

Acknowledgements

The author would like to acknowledge and thank all the working artists and hobbyists who have been
quoted, appear or assisted in creating this book.

The author and the publisher are grateful to the following for permission to reproduce copyright material:

Cover photograph: Maestro Bissolotti closing the case of a violin at his studio in Cremona, Italy, courtesy of
David Lees/CORBIS.

Wedding Chapel IV, 1960 (painted wood), Nevelson, Louise (1900-88)/Private Collection/Bridgeman Art
Library, p. 11; Coo-ee Picture Library, p. 26; Corbis, pp. 4 (bottom right), 7, 10, 12, 13, 14, 15, 16 (both), 18,
19, 21; Rob Cruse, pp. 9 (top), 9 (middle), 25; Istock, p. 4 (top); Cheryl Jakab, p. 5; Lebrecht Arts & Music
Picture Library, p. 17 (both); Lonely Planet Images, p. 9 (bottom); Photodisc, p. 6; Photolibrary.com, p. 20;
STAX, DIDGEMAN, www.didgeman.com.au, p. 22; http://www.woodturningcenter.org, website design:
Galactic Graphics c.1995-2005, p. 24; www.wasteconverters.com.au, p. 27; Vic Wood, pp. 4 (bottom left), 23.

While every care has been taken to trace and acknowledge copyright, the publisher tenders their apologies
for any accidental infringement where copyright has proved untraceable. Where the attempt has been
unsuccessful, the publisher welcomes information that would redress the situation.

Please note

At the time of printing, the Internet addresses appearing in this book were correct. Owing to the dynamic
nature of the Internet, however, we cannot guarantee that all these addresses will remain correct.

Contents

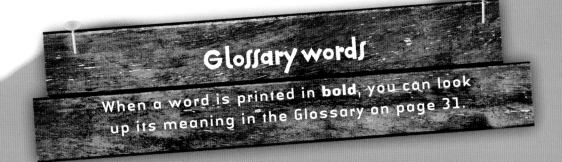

Glossary words

When a word is printed in **bold**, you can look up its meaning in the Glossary on page 31.

Wood artists

▼ African tribes have made masks from wood for hundreds of years.

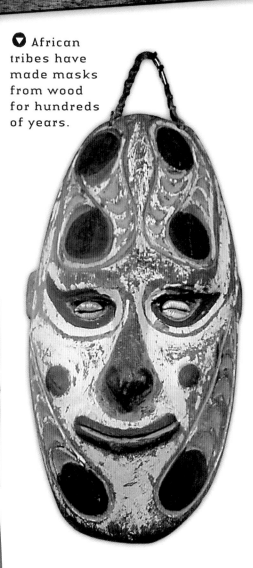

Look at these different artworks made by wood artists. Wood artists are people who design and make artworks with wood. Wood artists make a wide variety of items using a range of timbers, including:

- ▸ hand-crafted furniture
- ▸ totem poles
- ▸ masks and statues
- ▸ useful and decorative cups, bowls and plates
- ▸ musical instruments such as violins and guitars
- ▸ carvings on wall panels, chariots and boats.

▼ Totem poles are carved from one long piece of timber.

▼ Wood artwork can be polished so that it is smooth to the touch.

4

⬤ This wooden bowl, made by wood hobbyist Marion Williams, shows the texture of the wood used.

Using wood

Wood artists are people who are very skilled at shaping or joining selected pieces of wood. In this book, you will find the answers to these questions and more:

▶ What does a wood artist do?

▶ What do wood artists need to know about wood to use it creatively?

▶ How does wood help the artist express their ideas?

▶ What is it that artists like about wood as a **medium** for their art?

`I love the detailed patterns you find inside large tree burls [a type of growth found on tree trunks]. I cut then polish burls with power tools and by hand to a glossy finish.´
Marion Williams, school teacher and wood hobbyist

What is wood?

Wood is any of the hard parts from a tree. Wood includes the trunk, branches, stems or the veins in leaves. Even nuts and seed pods can be described as wood. Wood from different types of tree vary in pattern, colour, density and hardness. There are as many varieties of wood as there are of tree.

○ Some trees add one growth ring each year.

Patterns in wood

Growth rings and knots create patterns in wood. As a tree grows it becomes thicker. It does this by laying down new wood on the outer edge of the trunk and branches. This growth creates rings.

Knots in wood are areas where the trunk has grown around a branch. When the wood is cut, the knot can be seen as an irregular pattern in the **grain**. Knots create interesting patterns and colour in wood.

Softwood and hardwood

Wood can be either softwood or hardwood. 'Hardwood' comes from broad-leaved trees, such as oak, eucalypts and mahogany. 'Softwood' comes from trees with needle-like leaves, such as pine, casuarina and spruce. Hardwoods have a fine grain appearance. Softwoods usually have a similar surface to each other and often have a great deal of resin in them.

Woods have their own textures, colours and fragrances. Wood artists use different woods for different purposes.

Common woods

	Examples	Tree description	Characteristics	Uses
Hardwoods	oak	large tree from the beech family with acorn fruits	• very hard wearing • fine-grained	• barrel making • veneers • flooring • bridge girders • panelling
	mahogany	tropical tree found in Africa and America	• dark-reddish colour • strong • heavy • easily worked	• furniture • building materials (before the largest trees were all cut down)
	blackwood	large tree that grows in Eastern Australia	• golden brown to reddish brown with dark streaks • very hard	• furniture
Softwoods	pine	evergreen tree which can be fast-growing	• pale-yellow colour • grainy	• building materials or furniture (depends on species)
	cedar	evergreen tree with a red trunk	• red-coloured • hard wearing • fragrant	• cabinet making • pencils • building materials

Wood work

Wood artists make use of the different characteristics of wood in their work. They try to give their works beauty using the natural variety of colours, textures and grain in wood.

Wood artists often become skilled in one or two techniques while working with different types of wood. Different techniques require different tools. Wood working techniques include:

Some wood artworks are small and very detailed.

- general carpentry such as sawing, drilling and planing
- expert carving with chisels, **augers** and sandpaper
- turning wood on a **lathe**
- joining, such as **tongue and groove** joins
- expert finishing, including polishing and **laminating**.

Creating with wood

Work in wood is direct, once a cut has been made in wood it cannot be unmade. The way wood has grown affects the timber, so each piece is different. The artist needs to work with these differences when creating with wood.

Advantages of working with wood

The advantages of working with wood are that it:

- is light, strong and flexible
- comes in a great variety of colours and textures
- is easily cut and joined
- can be bent into shape
- can be coloured with stains and paints
- can be polished to a smooth finish.

'Wood is organic and unpredictable. The way it has grown and the structure of the plant are recorded in the wood.'
Steve Horton, wood turner

◐ ◑ Wood artists can create just about anything with wood.

⬇ Making string instruments is a skill that takes years to learn.

Wood artists today

Many wood artists express their ideas using both traditional and new techniques. New ideas can develop as a trend and are adopted by other artists or even used in mass-produced items.

Changes in working with wood

Wood artists are discovering new timbers to explore using traditional techniques. The technique for making string instruments has not changed for hundreds of years. The sound a violin or mandolin makes can change depending on the type of wood it is made from. The front of the violin is usually made of **well-seasoned** spruce and the back is made of maple. Some of the best violins being made today are based on traditional designs, but with new timbers.

New techniques

Artists today are still fascinated by the traditional ways of working wood but are also developing new techniques. Power tools for example, make working wood easier. Throughout the 1900s, artists working with wood maintained traditional designs using power saws, lathes, drills and sanders. Many modern wood sculptures show the grains and textures of the wood.

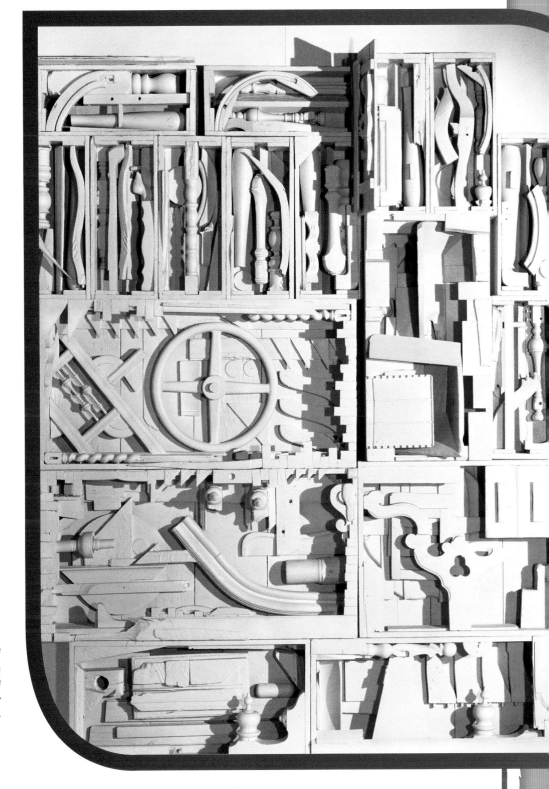

▶ This sculpture 'Wedding Chapel IV', was created by Louise Nevelson, a Russian-American sculptor.

'The grain of wood plays a part [in the sculpture] and makes it alive.'
Henry Moore, English sculptor

Wood turning

Wood turning is a wood-shaping technique that involves rapidly turning wood against a cutting tool. The machine that turns the wood is called a lathe. Lathes can be used to turn items such as table legs, bowls and posts.

To turn a piece of wood, the artist mounts the block of wood to the lathe, attaching it with screws at one end. As the lathe turns the piece of wood, the artist presses the cutting tool against it. The artist controls how quickly the lathe turns and the depth and angle of the cutting tool. This allows the artist to shape wood evenly and accurately.

▶ The harder the artist presses, the deeper the tool will cut.

Finishing

After the shape is complete, the artist can then use the lathe to finish the surface of the piece. First they sand the piece by holding a piece of sandpaper against the wood as it turns on the lathe. This achieves a smooth, even surface. The artist then applies a coating such as wax or lacquer while the piece is turning. This ensures that the piece is evenly coated and smooth.

Wood art history

It is difficult to know when woodwork began as an art form. Much of what has been made from wood in the past has rotted away. Wood was a major material for artwork until the 1800s when metals began to replace wood for many uses.

Tools

Many tools used for working wood today have been used since ancient times. These include saws, chisels, rasps, **planes** and the wood lathe. The way the lathes are powered has developed greatly through time. The earliest woodworking lathes, powered by rotating a pole, were developed around 600 BCE. These pole lathes were replaced by foot-powered lathes in the 1300s. Lathes were later powered by water, steam and electricity. Modern lathes work on the same principle as ancient lathes but are capable of more precise shaping and have improved power sources.

◀ The figurehead of this Maori longboat has been carved from wood by using saws and chisels.

Great wood traditions

Some woodworking traditions stand out due to the skill of the artists.

Gothic wood carving

In the 1400s and 1500s in Europe, many of the elaborate furnishings of churches were hand carved out of wood. In France, Germany and Spain, carved panels of wood told a story and were set in elaborate frames. The Belgian cities of Antwerp, Brussels and Malines were famous centres for these 'retables' and exported them all over Europe. This carved wood was also used to decorate buildings other than churches.

▶ This French gothic staircase at Leeds Castle, England, is carved in oak.

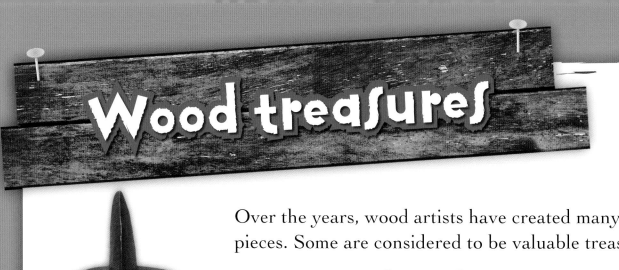

Wood treasures

Over the years, wood artists have created many different pieces. Some are considered to be valuable treasures.

Ceremonial masks

Masks are an example of classic African artwork. Masks are made to be worn in performances. The mask is often part of a costume combining wood with paint and textiles. The mask itself can have a range of meanings depending on local culture.

◄ This ceremonial mask was made in the Ivory Coast, West Africa.

Totem poles

Totem poles mean different things to different groups. In native American culture, they are carved emblems and sometimes show gods and animals. These tall poles, carved from wood, are like a family crest or family tree. Each 'totem' on the pole represents a family. Indigenous Australians use totem poles in ceremonies.

◄ Each totem on this native American totem pole looks different due to the use of colour.

🔺 Antonio Stradivari

Stradivari violins

Violins made by Antonio Stradivari between 1700 and 1725 are said to be the finest ever made. His violins are more sought after than those of any other instrument maker. Hundreds of his violins still exist today. Some experts believe the varnish he used was important in creating the great sound they produce. Violin makers are still trying to match the sound of Stradivari violins.

Antonio Stradivari had a long career at the Cremona school of violin makers in Italy. Stradivari worked under the great master Andrea Amanti, who may have been the inventor of the violin. During his career, Stradivari made many changes to the proportions of violins. He was still making instruments when he was in his nineties.

🔺 Some violins by Stradivari are over 300 years old and are sold for a lot of money.

CASE STUDY

Ancient Egyptian woodcraft

Around 2500 BCE, ancient Egyptian carpenters were experts in creating fine works in wood. Wooden objects were often expensive and available only to the rich. Wood artists were valued workers and were paid very well for their products. Artists carved items such as headrests, caskets and even make-up boxes for noblemen and women. Artworks were often decorated with carvings of animals such as lions, goats and snakes. Many wooden items and paintings of woodworking have been preserved in Egyptian tombs. More examples of ancient Egyptian woodworking tools and furniture are still being discovered today.

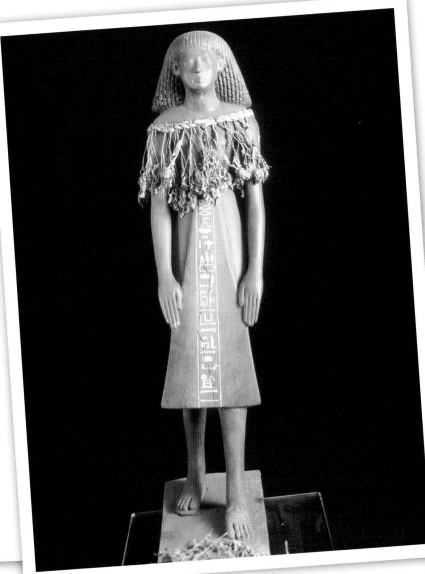

▶ Many ancient Egyptian wood carvings are kept in museums.

Types of wood in ancient Egypt

Wood was in very short supply in Egypt. Most of the wood had to be imported from other countries.

Wood	Source	Uses
date palm	Nile valley	• roof timbers
acacia	Nile valley	• pegs and dowels for joining
tamarisk	Nile valley	• walking sticks
sycamore fig	Nile valley	• coffins • chests • statues
cedar	Lebanon	• boats • building materials • furniture
ebony	Southern Africa	• furniture • statues

Woodworking tools

Ancient Egyptian woodworkers used various saws, knives and choppers to carve wood. After carving, stones were used to give the wood a polished finish. Ancient Egyptians also used a type of drill worked by a bowstring (the bow drill). Expert workers used these tools to create products that were highly valued in ancient Egypt.

▼ Tools such as these were once used in ancient Egypt.

Where wood artists work

▼ A wood artist's workshop can also be used to store finished artworks.

The wood artist s workshop is sometimes a large shed or garage with space and light. Depending on the type of work they do, the artist may need a wide range of hand or power tools. Many have both. Many types of tools such as saws, chisels, planes and files are often stored on walls with a special place for each item. Larger tools such as lathes are also kept in the workshop.

A vacuum cleaner or dust extractor is a useful addition to the wood artist's workshop. Wood dust and shavings need to be collected from the work area regularly. Breathing in too much wood dust can be bad for your lungs. Dust can also stick to painted or varnished artworks. Shavings are slippery and can be dangerous to leave on the floor Most workshops also have a wood storage area where wood can be kept flat and dry.

CASE STUDY
Studio woodwork

Studio woodworking is the crafting of wood by hand. After the invention of power tools in the 1800s, making wooden items by hand declined in popularity. Furniture was being made in factories and much of it was made of metal. During the 1950s, wood artists rediscovered working timber by hand and gave it the name 'studio woodwork'.

George Nakashima
(1905–1990)

George Nakashima was a well-known studio wood furniture maker who set trends in **contemporary** design. Nakashima was a Japanese–American who first trained as an architect. He worked with the famous American architect Frank Lloyd Wright. Nakashima made limited numbers of original furniture using carefully selected timbers like walnut and cherry.

⬥ George Nakashima with some of his chair and table designs.

Showing wood artworks

It is important for wood artists to show and sell their work. This is because they need to sell items in order to afford to continue working as an artist. It also gives people the chance to see the talent of the artist.

Wood artists can show their work in a studio, shop, gallery or online. Many wood artists' groups have regular shows where artists can exhibit their works. They can also attend workshops and view the works and techniques of others.

Wood artists who make larger items need to have their own studio, as moving large items to display elsewhere can be expensive. Many traditional wood artworks can now be seen on websites.

◀ An online gallery in a website can display a large amount of artwork—more than an exhibition space can.

Making a living as a wood artist

⬤ This wooden bowl is an example of a production item.

Artists may sell their works directly from their own gallery or workshop. They can also work by commission. This happens when people seeing an artist's work want a similar piece for a particular space. They can ask the wood artist to create a piece especially for them. Some woodworkers also teach their art at schools and colleges, or to individuals.

Production items

Production items are all made to a similar pattern or design even though each piece of wood is different. Selling these production items means wood artists can afford to work on more individual pieces.

Wood artists who make these items can take them to markets to sell directly to the public. These can be handcrafted toys, ornaments and bowls. They are popular because each one is an individual piece with its own character.

Wood artists' groups

There are many groups that wood artists can join. Members can be expert craftspeople or people who just enjoy woodworking as a hobby. They join to learn about woodwork arts. There are even groups that teach the ancient craft of joining wood without using modern tools.

The Wood Turning Center is based in Philadelphia, United States of America and was formed in 1986. It is a not-for-profit international art gallery and resource centre. The Center has the biggest collection of turned wood objects in the world, which can be seen both in the gallery and online.

Online groups

Online groups and associations can display work, share ideas, deal with issues and even sell work over the Internet. This sharing of ideas electronically has had a major effect on woodwork artists. Techniques with wood that were being used by isolated groups can now be viewed and shared online by people all over the world.

◀ The Wood Turning Center website displays all kinds of turned wood artworks.

Issues for wood artists

Wood artists need to be aware of health, safety and environmental issues that can affect their work.

Health and safety

Wood lathes, chisels, saws and hammers can all be dangerous if used without considering health and safety. Cuts, noise, dust and splinters are constant dangers. Safety equipment needs to be worn while using these tools. Keeping tools in good, working condition is very important. Artists must take care with varnishes, polishes and paints which can damage skin and give off harmful fumes.

Environmental impacts

Wood artists need to consider the environmental impact of their work. Wood comes from trees and the loss of natural forests is a worldwide problem. Trees that have taken hundreds of years to grow are becoming rare. Plantation, weed species and recycled timber are becoming more popular with wood artists for this reason.

▲ The tools used to work with wood can be harmful if you are not aware of health and safety issues.

The Artist Speaks

'Camphor Laurel is now recognised as an Australian noxious weed. Making use of it in furniture manufacture is an environmentally friendly pursuit.'
Brad McNab, timber artist

CASE STUDY
Recycling wood

In 2003, the Victorian Woodworkers Association (VWA) organised a competition called 'Create with a Crate'. The idea was to promote the re-use of timber that would otherwise go to waste. This is known as 'eco-recycling'. The challenge was to create artworks with wood from large wooden pallets used to import machinery. These are made of exotic timbers such as oak and elm.

'The difference between the mass produced object and the piece from the designer maker is pleasure for the buyer and satisfaction for the maker.'
Jane La Scala, Victorian Woodworkers Association member

◄ Wood from pallets can be reused by artists.

Fine timber used for pallets is often wasted, ending up in landfill. The competition aimed to change people's ideas about the uses of recycled wood and perhaps decrease the need for new timber. The competition produced a large variety of products.

Following on from 'Create with a Crate', in 2005 the VWA started a new competition. 'Woodworks' is an annual event showing the best in wood artwork. The competition is open to all artists, young and old.

It is hard to believe that these artworks were made from wooden pallets.

PROJECT
Make a polished wood coaster

What you need:

- a round or square piece of wood about 10 cm across and 1 cm thick
- sandpaper
- a piece of felt the size of the piece of timber
- gloves
- mask
- scissors
- glue
- linseed oil
- lint-free piece of cloth.

Pieces of wood cut across the grain and polished show decorative tree ring patterns. A large branch from a fruit tree, walnut tree or gum tree would be suitable for this project. Slices from these branches can be used to make coasters to put your drinks on.

You could even try using a smooth stone to finish the surface, like the ancient Egyptians did.

Sticking felt to the bottom makes the coaster suitable for use on good furniture.

What to do:

1. Put on the gloves and mask.

28

2. Rub the surface with the sandpaper, rubbing in the direction of the grain.

3. Polish the surface well by rubbing repeatedly with a peice of cloth. This will take time.

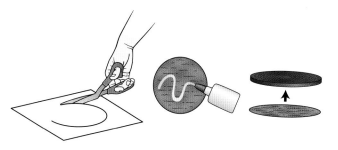

4. Pour a small amount of oil onto the cloth, and rub onto the finished surface.

5. Cut and glue the piece of felt to the bottom.

The Artist Speaks

'I use only natural oils on my pieces. Care of the finished product involves washing in warm soapy water and then re-oiling lightly.'
Steve Horton, wood artist

Wood art timeline

Before Common Era (BCE)

500 000   Wood used to make sharpened poles

30 000   Bow and arrow used for hunting

4000+   Bow drill and lathe first used in Middle East

3500   Solid wooden wheels used on carts; saws used to cut wood

2800   Plywood used in ancient Egypt

2500   Extensive use of woodworking tools in ancient Egypt; iron saw used in Mesopotamia

600   Greeks turn wood on pole lathes

100   Romans use iron cutters in tools such as wood plane and auger

Common Era (CE)

0   Romans develop the pump drill

1300s   Wheel spinning lathes developed in Europe, replacing the pole lathe

1500s   Thin strip metal saw used for intricate carving of hardwoods

1600s   Water driven mill saws used to cut wood

1712   Steam engine power becomes available

1789   Steam operated precision lathe invented

1830s   European cabinet makers use plywood

1840s   Turret lathe invented

1890s   Cheap plywood furniture produced

1950s   Computer operated tools introduced

Glossary

augers tools for boring holes in wood

contemporary belonging to the present time

grain the pattern in wood formed by growth rings in the trunk or branch

laminating making something by putting one layer on top of the other

lathe a machine that rotates items to be worked by stationary tools

medium material used

planes tools for removing thin layers of a piece of wood

tongue and groove a join in two pieces of wood created by pushing one piece into a hole in the other piece

well-seasoned wood that has been cut for some time

Index

Ancient Egyptian
Children

Richard Tames

Heinemann
LIBRARY

www.heinemann.co.uk/library

Visit our website to find out more information about **Heinemann Library** books.

To order:

☎ Phone 44 (0) 1865 888066

▤ Send a fax to 44 (0) 1865 314091

▣ Visit the Heinemann Bookshop at www.heinemann.co.uk/library to browse our catalogue and order online.

First published in Great Britain by Heinemann Library, Halley Court, Jordan Hill, Oxford OX2 8EJ, part of Harcourt Education Ltd. Heinemann is a registered trademark of Harcourt Education Ltd.

Editorial: Nick Hunter and Jennifer Tubbs
Design: Jo Hinton-Malivoire and Tinstar Design
(www.tinstar.co.uk)
Illustrations: Art Construction and Geoff Ward
Picture Research: Maria Joannou and
Virginia Stroud-Lewis
Production: Viv Hichens

Originated by Ambassador Litho Ltd
Printed in Hong Kong, China by
Wing King Tong

ISBN 0 431 14551 2
06 05 04 03 02
10 9 8 7 6 5 4 3 2 1

British Library Cataloguing in Publication Data
Tames, Richard, 1946 –
    Ancient Egyptian Childen. – (People in the Past)
    305.2'3'0932

Acknowledgements
The publishers would like to thank the following for permission to reproduce photographs: AKG London: pp.**6**, **9**, **11**, **16**, **22**, **26**, **32**, **36**, **40**, **41**; Ancient Art and Architecture Collection: pp.**10**, **15**, **17**, **20**, **28**, **34**, **43**; British Museum: pp.**7**, **30**, **31**; CM Dixon: p.**14**; Michael Holford: pp.**8**, **12**, **18**, **29**; Phil Cooke and Magnet Harlequin: pp.**5**, **24**, **42**; Scala Art Library: p.**38**.

Cover photograph of an ancient-Egyptian jug decorated with a mother and child reproduced with permission of AKG London.

The publishers would like to thank Dr Christina Riggs for her assistance in the preparation of this book.

Every effort has been made to contact copyright holders of any material reproduced in this book. Any omissions will be rectified in subsequent printings if notice is given to the publishers.

Contents

Words appearing in the text in bold, **like this**, are explained in the Glossary.

Land of the pharaohs

The amazing **civilization** of ancient Egypt was built along the banks of the River Nile. At 6670 kilometres (4145 miles), the Nile is the longest river in the world. Each year the melting of the snows in the mountains of Ethiopia caused the Nile to flood. Far away to the north in Egypt, the flooding river spread a layer of fertile black silt on the land for about 10 kilometres on either side. This narrow strip widened to 250 kilometres (155 miles) in the **delta** where the river split into many channels as it made its way into the Mediterranean Sea.

Civilization by the Nile

The annual flooding of the Nile renewed the fertility of the fields. The river provided the Egyptians with ducks, geese and fish for food. It also aided the growth of **flax** to be made into **linen** cloth, and reeds and **papyrus** for writing on and making into boats, baskets and sandals. The Nile also served as the country's main transport system. River transport made it possible to move around the huge quantities of stone needed to build the massive pyramid tombs of the pharaohs (kings) who ruled the land. The ancient-Greek **historian** Herodotus called ancient Egypt 'The Gift of the Nile' because it was the riches of the river that made the country great.

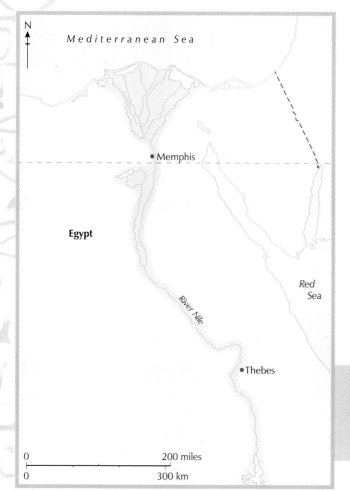

Mediterranean Sea

N

Memphis

Egypt

River Nile

Red Sea

Thebes

| 0 | 200 miles |
| 0 | 300 km |

This map shows the course of the River Nile as it runs through Egypt towards the Mediterranean Sea.

The Colossi of Memnon is the name given to these gigantic stone statues. Although damaged by wind, sand and frost, they have survived the last 3350 years. They were built under the instruction of Pharaoh Amenhotep III.

Egypt was rich in **copper** that could be made into tools, and in gold that could be made into jewellery and traded. There was abundant stone for building temples and tombs, and flint for making into knives, **sickles** and war clubs. Timber for making boats and furniture was in short supply and much had to be bought in from abroad.

The people of Egypt

Thanks to its rich resources ancient Egypt was able to support a population of up to 5 million people, and to create a civilization which lasted for over 3000 years. The Egyptians often lived short lives and many children died when they were still young. This book looks at the evidence that survives to tell us about the children of ancient Egypt, and explores what it can tell us about their lives.

Black land and red land

The Egyptians called their country after the colour of its rich soil – *Kemet*, which means the 'black land'. For them black meant good or lucky. Either side of the fertile corridor of the Nile valley lay hot, windy *Deshret*, the desert or 'red land'. The Egyptians believed only devils and the dead lived there. Red was therefore a bad and unlucky colour. Desert made up nine-tenths of Egypt's territory and served as a barrier against foreign invaders. Most of Egypt's people lived around the river – on the black land.

Lost lives

Historians try to rebuild the past out of what people made or wrote. Most of what the Egyptians made is lost forever. Items made of the most common materials – wood or wax, clay or cloth, bone or leather – are most likely to be broken, burned or to rot away. The same is true of **papyrus** or parchment documents.

What has survived tells us much less about children than it does about adults. Children had far fewer possessions than adults, and what they did have was not made to last. Adult possessions, like tools, weapons or jewellery were made of stone or metal, and were much more likely to survive. Children could not write about their lives, as adults did. Most never learned to write, and those that did were no longer children by the time they could.

Surviving evidence
Despite these problems a huge amount of evidence has survived thanks to two particular features of ancient-Egyptian **civilization**. Egypt's hot, dry climate has preserved many items that would have mouldered away in a damp country. Also the Egyptians' firm belief in the **afterlife** led them to **mummify** bodies, bury them with their possessions and decorate their tombs with elaborate paintings and **inscriptions**. Some of these tombs have survived.

Made of stone, this sculpture is of one of the daughters of Pharaoh Akenaten. There is much less surviving evidence of ancient-Egyptian children than adults.

6

Records of poor children are rare, but these boys are shown helping with the grain harvest.

Children's tombs often contain favourite dolls, toys and feeding bottles. They also have inscriptions which show how sad their parents were that they died. Their skeletons sometimes show signs of accidents. Modern science can also tell from their bones and teeth how well they were fed, and whether they had any serious illnesses.

The rich and the poor

As with other ancient civilizations, we know far more about the lives of the few rich and powerful people than we do about those of the ordinary farmers, who were most of the population. The rich owned more possessions, and were more likely to be able to write or be written about. They could afford expensive burials, even for their children. Ordinary Egyptians could not. Most of what we know of the lives of ordinary people comes from the viewpoint of the people they worked for.

Brief lives

If we could add up the lives of all the people who ever lived in ancient Egypt the children would outnumber the adults. Ancient Egyptians did not have as many doctors and medicines as we do and life could be hard. Many children died before they were old enough to have children of their own. But we know much more about the lives of adults than of children.

Being born

'Take a wife while you are young that she may make a son for you It is right to make people. A man with many children is happy because people think well of him because he has them.'

Egyptians wanted large families, as the above advice from a scribe shows. The Pharaoh Ramses II is said to have had about 45 sons and about 40 daughters by at least 7 wives! Wives were expected to have one baby after another. A wife unable to have children thought she was cursed by the gods. Other women were sorry for her. If a girl died before she had any children of her own, people thought she had lived to no purpose.

Giving birth

When a woman had a baby she was normally helped by nurses and **midwives**. In ordinary families, these helpers would often have been members of the mother's own family. Egyptian women gave birth in a shelter made of poles and branches, roofed with reed matting. This was built on the roof of their house or in its courtyard or garden. They stayed there for fourteen days after the birth. This would have allowed them to give the new baby their full attention, and kept the mother free of housework. It may also have helped to cut down the risk of infection because they were separated from other members of the household at a time when both baby and mother were most likely to catch something.

Ivory wands such as this one were thought to give protection against harm. Pregnant women used them as charms to help them survive childbirth, protecting both mother and child.

8

A dangerous time

Childbirth was very risky. Having babies too soon greatly increased the chances that either the mother or the baby would die. Repeated childbirth often weakened mothers and increased the danger of later births. Egyptians believed that Seshat, the goddess of writing and arithmetic, decided at the moment of their birth how long a person would live. If a baby died when, or soon after, it was born it may have been thrown to the crocodiles, or left at the edge of the desert for hyenas to eat. Older babies who died might be buried under the house, wrapped in palm leaves or **linen**. Although some had food, lucky charms, necklaces or toys buried with them, they were rarely **mummified** in the same way as older children and adults.

About half of all mothers died by the age of 40, although they would have had children at a young age. Because husbands were often older than their wives, few men lived long enough to know their grandchildren.

The decoration and shape of this jug show a kneeling mother hugging her baby to her. Being a baby was risky and many did not manage to reach childhood.

Looking after mother and child

Women prayed to the goddess Taweret who brought babies to the childless. This goddess looked like a pregnant hippopotamus with the arms and legs of a lion, and the back and tail of a crocodile. Beds were often painted with pictures of Taweret and babies' feeding bottles were made in her shape.

Bringing up baby

The high rate of deaths among babies and small children made Egyptian parents anxious to protect them in any way they could. They made charms from garlic, honey and river fish. They said prayers every morning as they tied a protective **amulet** around the child's arm or neck. Babies were also kept close to their mother, either being carried on her hip, or in a **linen** sling on their back. Despite all their care it seems likely that most mothers had as many as eight or nine babies, but three or four babies might die in infancy (childhood). The rest survived to reach their teenage years at least.

Babies were usually breast-fed until they were three. This is very much longer than would be normal in modern times, but it was common practise and had its advantages. Being breast-fed was much more hygienic and therefore safer than eating regular food. It is now known that when Egyptian infants were switched to solid food at the age of three, their death-rate rose sharply as a result of stomach infections.

In a garden, sorting fruit, this woman holds a child in a sling. It was common for babies to be strapped close to their mother or nurse in this way.

Pharaoh Akhenaten and his wife Nefertiti sit with their three daughters. The young children to the right are shown with shaved heads and the central girl has a **sidelock**.

Wet nurses

The wives of pharaohs and very wealthy men did not breast-feed their babies themselves. Instead they hired **wet nurses** to do this for them. Wet nurses were paid in goods such as necklaces, combs, sandals, baskets and cooking oil.

The wet nurse of a pharaoh's child might be the wife of a general or some high official, and she was treated with great honour. Paintings of royal people often include their wet nurse. Sometimes the wet nurse was kept on as a nanny. When royal infants grew up they usually thought of the children of their wet nurse as being like their own brothers and sisters, and so would help them get good jobs or husbands.

Naming the child

Immediately after birth a baby was named by its mother in case it died soon afterwards. This would explain such as names 'Welcome to you', 'She belongs to me', 'It is our sister', 'This boy I wanted' and 'The pretty girl has joined us'. Most names would have referred to a god or goddess. Daughters were often given the same name as their mother. For this reason many also had a nickname to make clear who was who. Babies might also be called after a member of the royal family. There is a woman's name, 'Beni', which literally means 'Sweetie'.

Home life

Most Egyptians lived in riverside villages. Children played close to home to be safe from the crocodiles and hippos that lived along the banks of the river. Snakes and scorpions were common in the desert land. Most homes were single-storey houses built of bricks. Bricks were made by mixing sticky river mud with chopped-up straw. Even children could help pack this mixture into wooden moulds and take the bricks out after they had dried in the sun.

The entrance to the home was also the family chapel, with offerings, like models of Egypt's gods, and busts of **ancestors**. The main room usually had an earthenware bench around the walls, for sitting and sleeping on. There were smaller sleeping and storage rooms off this. Cooking and messy jobs were done out in the courtyard, a safe area for infants to play in. The lavatory was a stool over a sand-pit. Thick walls kept houses cool, and also provided room for niches to store or display things in. In hot weather the whole family slept on reed mats on the flat roof.

A clay model of an ancient Egyptian house. Food is laid out in front of the home. This is where children would have played.

Drinking beer

Children as well as adults drank beer made from barley. It was thick and sweetened with spices, dates or honey. One tomb painting shows a child with a bowl and writing saying, 'Give me some beer because I am hungry.'

Rich people's homes had wall-torches or lamps to give light. There was not much furniture. The main items were wooden-framed beds, folding or fixed stools, low tables and chests for storage. Wealthy homes had gardens with flowers, fruit, vegetables and herbs, trees for shade and a pool for fish and watering the plants. Children would have spent much of their time outside.

Food and drink

Both rich and poor Egyptians alike lived mainly on bread, fish and vegetables, often made into stews, soups or porridge. **Archaeologists** have found remains of over 40 different kinds of bread, cake or biscuit. Some were flavoured with salt, honey, spices or fruit. Some had a hole which could be filled with an egg or beans.

The poor ate only at sunrise and dusk. The rich often ate in the afternoon as well. Bread flour was often coarsely ground with bits of stone or sand left in it. As a result even children as young as ten might have badly worn teeth. A mixture of honey and herbs was used to soothe toothache. Poor children ate meat only at religious festivals or family celebrations. The children of the rich ate meat often. Poor children ate dates as their sweetener, while the wealthy used honey.

Looking good

◄► ◄► ◄► ◄► ◄► ◄► ◄► ◄► ◄► ◄► ◄► ◄► ◄► ◄► ◄► ◄► ◄► ◄

Egyptian paintings usually show children naked. Most children probably were naked in summer, but not all the time. Artists showed them naked to make it clear they were children, and to distinguish them from adults. Children can also be identified by their hairstyle – the head shaved, with a piece of hair hanging down as a **sidelock**. Shaving the head prevented infestation by head lice.

From the age of about twelve children were expected to wear some clothes, summer and winter. The world's oldest surviving garment is a pleated **linen** shirt made for an Egyptian child around 2800 BC, and now in the Flinders Petrie Museum in Oxford. It had detachable sleeves to be sewn on for cold weather. Men wore a short **kilt**, knotted or buckled at the waist. Women wore tunics and are shown in tube dresses with either one or two shoulder straps in paintings. Labourers just wore a **loincloth**. Cloaks, shawls, **tunics** and furs were worn in winter.

Ancient Egyptian people liked to dress the hair of children into a sidelock. The child sitting on the adult's lap has her hair arranged in this way.

14

Linen clothes

Most people wore clothes of linen, made up at home. Most children's clothes would have been made by their mothers. Linen was light, cool and easy to wash and dry in the hot sun. Making linen was a long business, but the early stages were simple enough for older children to be able to help out with. **Flax** plants were gathered by hand, tied in bundles, dried out, combed to take out the seed capsules and soaked in water to separate out the fibres. These were then beaten to soften them, washed and then spun into yarn. Finally the yarn was woven into cloth. Linen was difficult to dye, so most garments were left plain.

Children and countryfolk often went barefoot. Better off people wore sandals of leather, or woven reed or grass. Children and men, as well as women wore jewellery. They also wore many **amulets**, which were charms to guard against evil.

Royal children

Members of the royal family were expected to look as splendid as the gods. The tomb of the boy pharaoh Tutankhamen was stuffed with clothes, including over 50 shirts and shawls, 30 gloves and over 100 triangular loincloths. There were also caps, belts, scarves and sandals. A baby's robe found with him was made of linen so fine it must have taken over 3000 hours to make.

In the tomb of the workman Inkerhau, at Deir el-Medina, this painting of the dead man and his family was found. The adults wear white linen garments. The children are shown naked apart from some items of jewellery.

Family life

The ancient Egyptians believed that death was only an interruption of life rather than the end of it. They thought of the family as consisting of dead relatives as well as the living. Even quite ordinary homes often had busts of **ancestors** on display. They were a constant reminder to children of family members they were too young to have known, but who were still watching what they did from the **afterlife**. Tomb paintings can mislead us into thinking that Egyptian households normally had many children because they show the ones who died as well as those who lived.

Children were valued because they would look after their parents in old age, when they were too feeble to look after themselves. It was just as important to the Egyptians that they should continue to look after them when they were dead. This meant making sure that their parents' tombs were built and that they were buried according to Egyptian customs.

Egyptian families preferred to have boys rather than girls. All children were thought of as a blessing. However, boys were valued more highly because they could be heads of their own households when they grew up.

This sculpture was made in about 1550 BC. By showing this family group with their arms around each other, the artist suggests they were close and loving.

Arranging funerals

The eldest son played an important part in his parents' funerals. When people wrote a **will** it often said that their surviving children had to pay for their funeral before they could inherit anything. A dead person could only enter the afterlife if funeral ceremonies had been performed properly. Once they had entered the afterlife the dead needed their surviving relatives to bring offerings of food and drink to their tombs to enable their souls to live on.

Girls were married off to the sons of other families, and this meant they were not there to look after their own ageing parents. So it made sense to marry girls off as soon as possible because the older they got the more they cost to feed and clothe. Fourteen was the usual age of girls when they got married. It was thought men should marry by the age of twenty. Many cousins married each other. Often men married their nieces.

Seneb, a dwarf, sits with his wife, Senetites, and their two children. The children have been made to look much smaller than the adults and have fingers in their mouths. Artists often exaggerated the small size of children, but as Seneb was an adult he is seated on a block to make him appear as tall as his wife.

Working at home

Wealthy people had **slaves** to do all their household work, so the children of rich parents did not have to help out around the home.

Most children did do some work from about the age of five. They began by looking after their younger brothers and sisters, running errands, fetching water from the river or from a nearby well. They also helped with sweeping up, and carrying food out to people working in the fields of their village.

The harvesting of crops was a very important part of ancient-Egyptian life. Much food needed to be grown to keep everyone fed. Children picked up grain that was dropped by the men who carried it from the fields to a threshing floor. They would take the grain home for their families. Oxen would walk over the crops collected by the men to separate the stalks from the ears.

In Egyptian art women are normally shown as paler than the men because they were expected to spend more time indoors, out of the fierce sunlight. Baking bread and brewing beer were done daily because neither would keep for long. Girls would learn how to do these essential chores by helping their mothers. As they got older they would master the other endless task, making **linen** and weaving it into cloth. Basket-weaving was another important skill. Grasses, **papyrus** and palm leaves were all used to make baskets and chests for storing food and clothes. They were also used as matting for floor coverings and roofing. Herbs were grown close to the house for use in cooking and making medicines.

Working in the fields

Farm work was the most common way of making a living. Tomb paintings often show children joining in. In the spring young boys helped to clean out **irrigation ditches** and drive the livestock across the fields to trample in seed. Children also helped to scare away birds from eating the growing crops by shouting and throwing stones. They also had curved sticks, like boomerangs, which were thrown at birds in flight to bring them down. After the harvest children searched the fields, picking up fallen scraps of grain. Because wood was very scarce and expensive to burn on the fire children were also sent to gather animal droppings that were dried out in the sun to be used for winter fuel.

The sons of craftsmen or artists followed in their father's trade. Because so much of Egypt was desert, there was a shortage of timber. This meant that furniture-makers learned how to disguise poor quality wood by covering it with ebony or ivory. Glassmakers also recycled broken items to turn them into **amulets**, beads or containers for cosmetics. Interestingly while it is quite common for paintings of farm work to show children helping out, they are not included in pictures showing craftsmen at work.

Working away

Many Egyptian farmers were **serfs**, tied by law to the land of their village – which made them sure of work and food. A farmer's daughters were more likely than his sons to leave their village. They usually left to get married, although there were some jobs open to females – servant, weaver, baker, musician, dancer, **wet nurse** and laundress.

These craftsmen are preparing to build a ship. The sons of craftsmen would normally learn their father's trade.

Egyptian ideas about work

This saying from the **New Kingdom** period tells us what the Egyptians thought about children working: 'You shall not spare your body when you are young; food comes about by the hands, provision by the feet.' This means that children had to work hard if they wanted to eat!

If a craftsman had several sons they might all learn his trade, but some might need to move to a city to find work. Boys who wanted to be soldiers went to work in a **fort**. They began by helping **grooms** look after **chariot** horses, and cleaning soldiers' weapons and equipment.

Servants

Rich families in ancient Egypt often employed servants. They would have worked in the kitchen and around the house. Many of these servants would have been young people who had been sent out to earn money because their families could not afford to support them. Girls would probably have married when they were in their early teens. Those who were not married often left home to work as maids for wealthy women. They would have lived on the estates where they worked, and would have seen their own families only rarely, if at all.

Slavery

Slaves were not as numerous as in ancient Greece or Rome. Most were foreigners, Nubians from the south, or people from the Near East. Slaves were usually either captured as prisoners of war, or were the children of people who had been captured or bought from slave traders. Slave traders either bought or kidnapped people in their home countries. Some people sold themselves and their children into slavery because it was the only way they could pay off their debts.

School

The Egyptian system of writing with **hieroglyphs** took many years to learn. At most only one or two children in every hundred learned to read and write well. Being **literate** was a passport to a top job as a government official, army officer, scribe or priest. The importance of literacy in ancient Egypt can be seen from the many surviving statues that show a person with writing equipment.

This statue shows a young male in the typical pose of a scribe. He pulls his **kilt** tight across his legs so that he has a surface to support his papyrus. Young scribes practised writing on boards, but experienced scribes wrote on papyrus scrolls. Scribes were also taught to do maths, so that they could work out taxes.

Advice for scribes

Schooling was not meant to be enjoyable. The scribe Amenemope warned his son, 'pass no day in idleness or you will be beaten. The ear of a boy is on his back. He listens when he is beaten.'

He also told his son why it was worth putting up with school, 'No scribe is short of food and of riches from the palace.' Scribes did not pay taxes or have to work on building projects either. The alternatives were much worse – 'I have seen the smith at work at the opening of his furnace … he stinks more than fish roe … the potter … grubs in the mud more than a pig!'

There was a school attached to the royal court where the pharaoh's children were taught. Sometimes this might include girls as well, though normally only boys went to school. Other pupils at the court school would be children of foreign rulers under Egyptian control, and children of the pharaoh's generals, officials and priests. Some children from ordinary families might also be sent there. Being at school with a future pharaoh gave such children the chance of a fine career in his service. Some temples also had schools, although there were no special school buildings. Classes were held in the open air.

Learning from books

Lessons were based on written textbooks that did not change for centuries. These books were not like our books – they were in fact long scrolls made up of several sheets of **papyrus**. Pupils were not expected to understand what they were writing until they were older. Learning things by heart was a very important skill, and so was learning to speak clearly and confidently. A man's speech could earn him favours. Egyptian boys were taught to keep calm at all times, and to think before saying or doing anything.

Reading and writing

Papyrus was expensive and so Egyptian children learned to write by practising on broken bits of pottery, which the Greeks called *ostraca*. *Ostraca* found at the workmen's village at Deir el-Medina show they were also used for everyday notes between neighbours. This means that skilled working men – sometimes even their wives too – could read and write a little. The son of a scribe, however, would master a whole range of standard documents and letters that he would have to write many times over in the course of his career.

Pictures and signs made up hieroglyphs. Although records were kept on papyrus, colourful hieroglyphs were written on walls. They were a sacred form of writing. Here, amongst other signs, owls, snakes and birds are used to make words.

Papyrus – the first paper

Most writing was done on papyrus. This was a paper made from strips of pith from a kind of reed that grew along the banks of the River Nile. Separate sheets of papyrus were stuck together in long rolls. The longest one to have survived, dating from around 1150 BC, measures 41 metres. Papyrus lasted for centuries providing it did not get damp. It could also be scraped clean for re-use.

Hieroglyphs

The most formal style of writing was known as *medu netjer*, which means 'divine words'. The Greeks translated this term as **hieroglyph**, meaning 'sacred writing'. Hieroglyphs were used on monuments and tombs. There were over 6000 hieroglyphs, though only a few hundred were in common use.

Some hieroglyphs were simplified pictures of what they referred to, such as a man or a loaf of bread. Others were pictures standing for sounds. A picture of a human foot represented the sound 'b'. All sound signs stood for consonants. There were none for vowels, which the reader was meant to put in on their own. Hieroglyphs could be written side to side or top to bottom. The oldest known hieroglyphic writing dates back to around 3200 BC. The last known hieroglyphic **inscription** dates from AD 394.

In addition to hieroglyphs there was a simpler script, known as **hieratic**, which read from right to left – the opposite way to this page. Hieratic could be written quickly, and was used for most daily purposes, especially writing documents

The main writing instrument was a reed, cut at the end to make a nib. Ink was made out of vegetable gum and soot. Scribes carried their pens and inks in special boxes.

Figure it out

Unlike the ancient Greeks, the Egyptians never thought of doing sums just for fun. The dimensions of the pyramids show, however, that they could measure distances and quantities with astonishing accuracy. The sides of the largest pyramid are 230 metres long, and differ from each other by only a few centimetres.

Practical Problems

Boy scribes probably only began to learn mathematics near the end of their training. They had to because it was useful. One use was for recording the taxes they collected. Another was working out how much they ought to collect next season. They did this by using knotted ropes to measure the area of land being farmed. They then used the 'Nilometer', marked scales located at different points along the Nile, to calculate the river's height, and estimate the strength of its annual flooding.

These two measurements enabled them to work out roughly how much food would be grown in an area, and therefore how much could be taken in taxes. A surviving mathematical text also shows how to work out how much grain a granary could hold.

This mathematical **papyrus** is called Papyrus Rhind. Calculations on it were made to work out how much grain could be fitted into a granary. On part of it, the scribe has done sums to divide some of the grain into fractions.

Different signs mean different amounts. These were put together to make larger numbers.

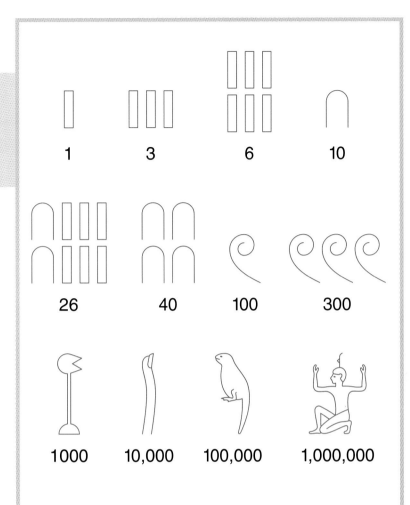

| 1 | 3 | 6 | 10 |

| 26 | 40 | 100 | 300 |

| 1000 | 10,000 | 100,000 | 1,000,000 |

Measuring

The Egyptians used the 'cubit' as their standard unit of measurement. The cubit was based on the length of a man's forearm, and would have been equal to 52.4 centimetres. The cubit was subdivided into seven palm-widths. Each palm-width equalled four thumb-widths.

Time

Most children had no need to tell the time accurately. They simply got up when it was light, and went to bed when it was dark. Those who did need to measure the passing of time used water-clocks. They had dip-sticks, which showed how much water had flowed out of the vessel and therefore how much time had passed.

Counting money?

Children did not need to know how to count money. Egyptians had no coins to use as money, but they did use weights of **copper** to calculate the value of different goods. This made it easier to work out how many woven baskets for example one should barter, or swap, for a jar of oil. Wages and taxes were usually paid in goods or produce such as barley, honey, **linen** or reed mats.

Toys

It is not always easy to be certain that what looks like an ancient-Egyptian toy actually is a toy. What look to us like dolls or puppets were often used for religious purposes, such as an offering to the gods, or for magic, to cast a spell. Many tombs contain *shabtis*, carved and painted wooden figures. These figures were meant to work as servants for the dead person in the **afterlife**. What look like toy boats and model houses or farms have also been found in the tombs of adults. These were clearly not meant to be toys, but are examples of what they would find or need in the afterlife.

Most children's toys were easily broken or destroyed over time by damp or fire, so few have survived. Some have been found intact in the tombs of young children. Others are illustrated in paintings. Family members made most toys. Children in rich families might have toys made by skilled craftsmen.

Toys for babies

Babies were given clappers or rattles made of dried **gourds**, wood, clay or bone. Some had metal bells or loose pebbles inside. Figures of farmyard or pet animals were made out of clay, wood or **bronze**. Dolls were made out of cloth and wax. They often had movable arms and legs and different sets of clothes for dressing up. Some dolls have been found with holes drilled into their scalp to take 'hair' made from fibres of **flax**.

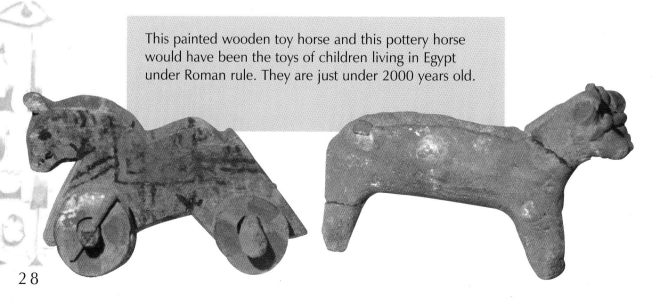

This painted wooden toy horse and this pottery horse would have been the toys of children living in Egypt under Roman rule. They are just under 2000 years old.

Older children played with whipping tops. These were usually made of wood, but some have been found made of clay and covered by 'faience' – a glass-like glaze. These would have been expensive to make, but were very pretty and would last much longer than wooden ones, as well as spinning better. Another luxury toy has been found consisting of a base, with little ivory figures on it which twirl around when a string is pulled.

Children in ancient Egypt would have played with toys like these two. A glaze on the doll makes her look turquoise. The cat has moveable jaws and bronze teeth. They were made in about 1450 BC and 1300 BC.

Children and pets

The problem of being sure just what was a toy also applies to pets because birds and animals were also offered to the gods. Egyptian children certainly kept cats, dogs and monkeys as pets as well as different kinds of birds such as ducks, pigeons, lapwings and hoopoes. However, pictures showing children with geese or gazelles are probably not showing them as pets. Geese can be very dangerous towards small children, and gazelles cannot be tamed.

Games and sports

In the countryside children could go swimming in **irrigation canals** and ride on donkeys. Although most fishing was done with nets or traps some was done by harpooning. This way of fishing was less certain of success, but more fun!

Ball games

Children played many games with balls made in different ways. The outer covering might be cloth, leather or **papyrus**, and the stuffing inside could be barley husks, straw, grass, rags, reeds or horsehair. Wooden balls were used to knock down skittles. Some skittle games were played by bowling the balls through gaps in a gateway before they hit the skittles. Girls favoured juggling, usually with three balls. The best could juggle while keeping their arms crossed. There were also girls' games that involved throwing and catching balls while clapping in between throws and catches.

The British Museum houses these rare ancient-Egyptian toys. Balls would have been used in games.

Egyptian paintings rarely show boys and girls playing together. Boys' games were sometimes rough. One, called 'jumping over the goose', needed two boys to sit facing each other with arms clasped together to make a barrier. As other boys jumped over their arms, they tried to catch a trailing foot to bring the jumper crashing down. Arm-wrestling and leap-frog were also popular. Most games were played by two, or only a few players. Tug-of-war was one of the few team games. To toughen them up for the army older boys did sports such as wrestling, fighting with the **quarterstaff** and target-shooting with a bow and arrows.

Senet

Both rich and poor children, and adults, played board games. The exact rules for their use are not known. The most popular game was 'Senet' ('passing'), that seems to have been like a complicated form of snakes and ladders. Each player usually had seven pieces that had to be moved along a grid of three rows of ten squares. Some of the squares were lucky and others were unlucky. Moves were decided by throwing sets of **knuckle-bones** which acted like dice. One Senet board, from the tomb of Tutankhamen, was made in the shape of a box, with a playing surface on top, inlaid with ivory. The ivory playing-pieces and knuckle-bones used in the game could be stored inside. The game could be played much more simply by scratching a board on stone or even in sand or dust, and using pebbles for counters.

Sickness and health

The death rate among babies and small children in ancient Egypt was very high. Infants often died from **dysentery**, a stomach infection caused by poor hygiene, such as drinking dirty water or eating unwashed fruit and vegetables. Where there was no obvious cause for illness, like a wound or insect bite, it was blamed on evil spirits. If evil spirits were suspected, a spell was said – 'Come on out, visitor from the darkness …. Have you come to kiss this child? I forbid you to do so! Have you come to harm it? I forbid this! I have prepared a potion to protect it, made from a poisonous herb, from garlic which is bad for you and honey which is sweet for the living but bitter for the dead.'

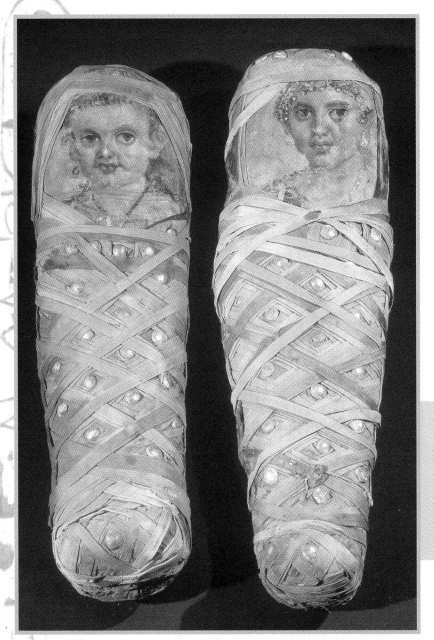

There are few surviving mummies of children, but some have been found. As with adult mummies, they are the bodies of children from rich.and influential families.

Clues from mummies

Mummifying so many bodies must have improved the Egyptians' knowledge of human **anatomy**. It certainly helps modern **archaeologists** to find out the kind of diseases that young Egyptians suffered from. Many suffered from lung diseases caused by the hot and dusty climate in which they lived.

Mothers also tried to protect their babies by tying written spells around their necks. These spells were supposed to ward off diseases and accidents. Bites from snakes and scorpions were a particular danger as children often walked around in bare feet. Cuts or burns that became poisoned could also lead to early death. Mothers were advised that a child with teething troubles should be fed a fried mouse!

Short lives

There are 26 royal **mummies** in the Egyptian Museum at Cairo. Because they were better fed and cared for, and less exposed to danger or fatigue than any other group the royal family should have had the best chances for a long life. X-rays show however that only Pharaoh Ramses II lived past the age of 55. Three more died between the ages of 40 and 50. All the rest died between the ages of 20 and 40. The bodies of nearly 300 ordinary people, dug up from a cemetery at Abusir, showed that their average age at death was between nineteen and twenty.

Egyptian doctors could mend broken bones with splints, and knew how to heal bad cuts with wound-packings, bandages and **poultices**. Along with these practical skills, they often used lucky charms and spells as part of their treatment. Poor children would probably not have been able to afford to see a doctor. They would have relied on magic, and the protection of the gods to keep them healthy.

Beliefs and behaviour

Although ancient Egypt was a rich land where people could live well, it also suffered from droughts, **epidemics** and invasions. It was normal for people to see many of their children die young. Perhaps for these reasons the Egyptians believed that the world ought to be unchanging and orderly. The goddess Maat, who stood for truth and justice, represented this idea. She also controlled the regular pattern of the stars and seasons. The task of the pharaoh was to rule as the servant of Maat. He did this by performing religious ceremonies to keep the gods in touch with the people. He also punished thieves, and defended Egypt against invaders.

Over the course of more than three thousand years Egypt was governed by 30 different **dynasties** of pharaohs. Peaceful rule was interrupted by wars, disasters and periods of disorder. Each time the Egyptians would rebuild their way of life under a new ruler on what they believed to be the same

A glazed hippopotamus statue of the goddess Taweret. She was thought of as goddess of childbirth. The statue was made in about 400 BC.

Advice for sons

This advice for the boys has been found:

'If a man's son accepts his father's words, his plans will not fail … When he is old and respected he will speak likewise to his own children, renewing the teaching of his father … he will speak to his children so that they in turn will speak to their children. Set an example … if Maat is upheld then your children will live … a dutiful son is a gift from heaven.'

old lines. Children were therefore brought up to follow the customs of the past. These would teach them how to behave correctly towards other family members, neighbours, guests, strangers, priests and officials of the pharaoh.

Winning favour

Boys were often named after their uncle or grandfather because he was a good person they ought to copy. Boys were brought up to believe that the greatest good fortune was to win royal favour by serving bravely as a soldier or working hard as a scribe. The pharaoh's closest servants were known as the 'king's sons' even when they were not related to him at all. A successful career meant getting a pleasant home and a good reputation. It also meant being able to look forward to being reborn in the **afterlife**.

Girls were brought up to be obedient, hard-working and silent. They should want to devote their life to their husband, and have many children. The goddess Isis was held up as the ideal wife and mother every girl should want to grow up into.

Holidays and festivals

The craftsmen who lived in the village of Deir el-Medina worked eight days out of every week of ten days. There were also between 50 and 75 public festivals a year, some lasting several days. This gave the craftsmen time off to do other things, such as hunting and fishing. They might take their older sons with them to teach them how to use a throwing-stick, or fish with a net.

Hunters scare birds into flight from a marsh in this tomb scene. On the left a man and child both have throwing-sticks. Hunting for birds in this way was a popular sport for rich Egyptians.

Horus as a child

The same god could take different forms and have different names. The important god Horus could be shown as a falcon, or a man with a falcon's head. He could also be shown as a child standing on a crocodile and surrounded by snakes, scorpions and other dangerous animals. Showing him as a child, with a **sidelock** and sucking his finger, was a way of reminding people he was the child of Isis.

When shown as a child Horus was known as Hor-Pa-Khered, or Harpocrates. An **amulet** with Harpocrates on it was supposed to protect the wearer from snake bites or scorpion stings.

Preparing for festivals

Festivals were held to honour the gods. Normally only priests were allowed to go inside temples at festival times, so the statues of gods were brought out. They were paraded around for all to see and ask favours from. Some were carried on portable **shrines**, others floated in specially built boats.

At various points in Egyptian cities and towns special stands were built and decorated, so that statues of the gods could rest and be seen by the people of that neighbourhood. Before a big festival took place there would be days of preparation. Boys would help their fathers to build neighbourhood shrines. Girls would help their mothers to decorate them with flowers and offerings of fruit, vegetables and lengths of home-made **linen**.

As well as the great temple and royal festivals, there were many local ones held at village and household shrines. These were to ensure that the family prospered, and the fields gave a good harvest. Priests used a special calendar based on the phases of the moon to work out when festivals should be held. Most followed the farmer's year, with celebrations to mark the ploughing and sowing of the fields, and later the gathering of their crops.

All grown up

Boy to man

In ancient Egypt, a priest performed a ceremony when boys were about fourteen to show that they had now grown up. Children would also stop wearing the **sidelock** hairstyle. The **mummy** of a young prince aged about eleven was found in the tomb of Pharaoh Amenhotep II.
The prince still wore a sidelock like a child. This tells us that he had not yet reached adulthood.

A banquet scene from the tomb of Ramses in Thebes. A rich family would probably have celebrated a marriage with such an event.

Advice for marriage

Scribes wrote down advice for married couples: 'Do not boss your wife … when you know she knows what she is doing … Do not say to her 'Where is it? Get it!' when she has already put it in the right place.'

Girl to woman

As soon as girls were old enough to have children of their own their family would begin to look for a husband for them. Marriage was a matter for the people involved and their families. The bride and bridegroom needed their parents' permission to get married, and sometimes drew up a legal agreement to set out their rights as husband and wife. This contract would be given to a third person, or stored in a temple for safe-keeping. The couple might live together for a year to see if the wife could have a baby. If the couple got **divorced** because there was no baby, the wife had a right to some of the property they had owned while they were together.

Egyptians had no wedding ceremony, and no special clothes or ring. The bride did not change her name. There was a noisy, happy procession of well-wishers to accompany the bride from her family home, to the home of her new husband. Egyptians loved to have a party, so there would have been a banquet as well. The groom gave the bride a small gift of cash and corn to show that he would provide for her. The bride's father often gave the newly-weds household goods and food. Surviving statues of married couples holding hands and accompanied by their children show that husbands and wives felt affection for each other, and pride in their sons and daughters. Because many women died in childbirth and older husbands often died before their wives, there were many single parent families. Remarriage was common, so many children had a step-father or step-mother.

Treasures of a boy king

When wealthy Egyptians died their tombs were filled with goods for them to use in the **afterlife**. Because royal tombs contained the finest things they were a target for tomb-robbers. When modern **archaeologists** began to **excavate** tombs they were disappointed to find that all the royal ones had been robbed of their contents.

Then, in 1922, English archaeologist Howard Carter discovered the tomb of Tutankhamen, a teenage pharaoh who had ruled for less than ten years around 1330 BC. His tomb had been forgotten about because it had been covered up by a deep layer of rock chippings made during the building of neighbouring tombs. Tutankhamen's tomb had been partly robbed twice, but sealed up again. It still contained his body, his gold coffins, gold funeral mask and many treasures in excellent condition.

Inside the tomb

Tutankhamen's body was wrapped in fine bandages, with many charms and jewels between the different layers. The body was then sealed up in a coffin of solid gold, inside two outer coffins of wood covered with beaten gold. Around it in his burial chamber were four wooden **shrines**, covered with gold and religious writings. Other rooms in the tomb were crammed with

Howard Carter (left) was the English archaeologist to find the treasures of the tomb of Tutankhamen. Being hidden from tomb robbers in the dry climate of Egypt preserved the coffins and mummy, alongside all the provisions for the afterlife that were buried.

clothes, a throne, three couches, food containers, statues, weapons and six **chariots**. There were also model boats, a model granary and dozens of wooden *shabti* dolls, intended to wait on the pharaoh as his servants in the afterlife. The **mummies** of two female children were buried with him. They were almost certainly his children that had not survived.

Because he was so young Tutankhamen probably had very little personal power. All the important decisions were made by his chief adviser, an old court official called Ay, and his top general Horemheb. Both ruled as pharaohs after Tutankhamen's early death. The survival of the boy king's tomb and treasures has made him the most famous pharaoh of all. However, he seems to have done little in his own short life to deserve such great fame.

The golden funeral-mask of the boy pharaoh Tutankhamen was found in the inner coffin. The boy is dressed as Osiris, god of the dead. He wears a blue and gold headcloth, a ceremonial beard and the images of a vulture and a cobra on his forehead.

How do we know?

The key to unlocking Egypt's past was the discovery in 1799 of a public notice known as the Rosetta Stone. This had an **inscription** carved on it in Greek, in a form of **hieratic** known as **demotic**, and also in **hieroglyphs**. Until the discovery of the Rosetta Stone no one knew how to read hieroglyphs. It took almost thirty years for scholars to work out how to interpret the hieroglyphs. Once this was done they could read the thousands of other Egyptian inscriptions and documents surviving from the past.

Discoveries can also be made by re-examining what we already have. The pleated garment referred to on page 15 was part of a bundle of rags that Sir Flinders Petrie brought back from excavations in Egypt in 1912. No one realised what it was until it was re-examined in 1977.

Tombs and chapels were built by the people of Deir el-Medina. They left food and drink for their ancestors, hoping to sustain them in the afterlife.

Nakht the weaver

New scientific methods help archaeologists learn far more from a **mummy** than they could in the past. In 1974, a team examined the body of a teenage **weaver** called Nakht who lived during the reign of Ramses III (about 1187 BC to 1156 BC). The way his leg bones developed show that he had worked for long hours in a cross-legged position. The tapeworm found in his stomach suggests he ate meat. The red **granite** dust in his lungs showed he lived near Aswan, the only place in Egypt where this stone is found. He probably died of a lung disease or stomach infection, or a combination of the two. Although his family could not afford to have him **mummified** properly, they had stuffed his body with two shirts to keep its shape, and wrapped it in a **burial cloth**. Nakht's short life seems to have been like that of many children of ancient Egypt. It was filled with hard work, and troubled by some pain but also remembered by his family with love.

Even after two centuries of **excavations** much remains to be uncovered. So far **archaeologists** have concentrated on temples and the tombs of the great Egyptians. The workmen's village of Deir el-Medina has revealed a very different side to life from what can be learned from Tutankhamen's tomb including the homes and belongings of workers and their families. We do not yet know how typical that settlement was. The many unexcavated possibilities for the future include looking under known sites, under modern cities, in the marshy Nile **delta** and in Egypt's thousands of villages and small towns.

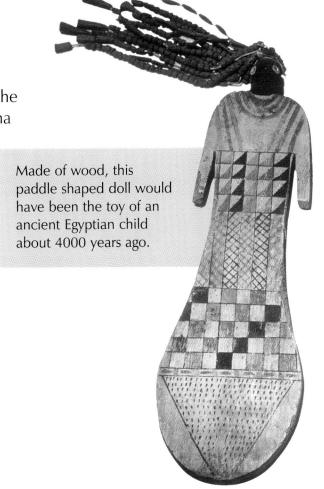

Made of wood, this paddle shaped doll would have been the toy of an ancient Egyptian child about 4000 years ago.

Timeline

All dates are BC. Pharaoh's dates refer to reigns.
All dates are approximate as they vary from source to source.

Before 5000
Early settlers farmed and built towns along the Nile.

About 3000
Menes unites Lower and Upper Egypt. Dynasties (ruling families) 1, 2 and 3.

2575 to 2130 The Old Kingdom
Great Pyramids are built at Giza.
Dynasties 4 to 8. Trading expeditions, war with Libyans.

2130 to 1938 First Intermediate Period
A time of weak rulers. Dynasties 9, 10 and 11.

1938 to 1600 Middle Kingdom
Power of pharaohs is restored. Dynasties 12 and 13.

1630 to 1540 Second Intermediate Period
Dynasties 14 to 17. Invasion of Hyksos. Egyptians face **chariots** for the first time.

1539 to 1075 New Kingdom
Dynasties 18 to 20. Egypt's power at its height. Reign of Akhenaten (Amenhotep IV) in the 1300s. Tutankhamen (1333 to 1323), the boy-pharaoh whose tomb later reveals much about Egyptian life. Ramses II (1279 to 1213) known as Ramses the Great.

1075 to 665 Third Intermediate Period
Dynasties 21 to 25. Pharaohs of Libyan heritage rule Egypt (dynasties 21 to 23). Dynasty 25 were Kushite rulers.

664 to 31, a time of foreign rule
Dynasties 26 to 30. Local rulers struggle for power. Dynasty 27 consisted of Persian kings who did not rule Egypt, but styled themselves as pharaohs. Dynasties 28 to 30 were native rulers. 332 Alexander the Great from Greece conquers the country. New dynasty, under Ptolemy, a Greek, is founded in 305. 51 Cleopatra becomes joint ruler of Egypt with her brother. She rules alone from 47.
31 Defeat by Roman fleet at sea battle of Actium ends Egypt's power. Romans make Egypt a Roman province.

Sources and further reading

Sources

A Dictionary of Ancient Egypt, Margaret Bunson
(Oxford University Press, 1995)

British Museum Dictionary of Ancient Egypt
(British Museum Press, 1995)

Growing Up in Ancient Egypt, R.M. and J.M.Janssen
(The Rubicon Press, 1990)

Mummies: Unravelling the Secrets of and Ancient Art, Bob Brier
(Michael O'Mara Books Limited, 1996)

The Egyptian Gods and Goddesses, Clive Barrett
(Diamond Books, 1996)

The Penguin Historical Atlas of Ancient Egypt, Bill Manley
(Penguin Books, 1996)

Further reading

Ancient Egypt, Jane Walker
(Miles Kelly, 2002)

Explore History: Ancient Egypt, Jane Shuter
(Heinemann Library, 2001)

What Do We Know About the Egyptians? Joanna Defrates
(Simon and Schuster, 1992)

Glossary

afterlife life after death

amulet lucky charm

anatomy study of the body

ancestor family member from long ago

archaeologist person who studies ancient objects to understand the past

bronze metal made by mixing tin and copper

burial cloth cloth used to wrap a dead body

chariot two-wheeled cart used for racing or warfare

civilization developed society

copper reddy-gold coloured metal used for tools, weapons, beads or bangles

delta river mouth split into smaller streams divided by islands

demotic simplified version of writing

divorce parting of a husband and wife, ending the marriage

dynasty ruling family

dysentery stomach infection causing the sufferer to go to the toilet often

epidemic large-scale outbreak of a disease

excavate dig up items from the past

flax plant whose fibres can be made into linen cloth

fort strong building with soldiers to defend an important place

gourd round plant which can be dried for use as a container or rattle

granite very hard kind of stone

groom person who looks after horses

hieratic shortened hieroglyphs use by priests

hieroglyphs symbols used for Egyptian writing

historian person who studies ancient documents to understand the past

inscription writing carved into a surface

irrigation ditch/canal channel dug to carry water to or from a field

kilt wrap-around, knee-length skirt

knuckle-bones bones from an animal's hand used as dice

linen light cloth woven from fibres of the flax plant

literate able to read and write

loincloth under-garment worn around the middle like shorts

midwife nurse who helps women to have babies

mummify to preserve a dead body as a mummy

mummy body preserved by removing internal parts, drying flesh with chemicals and then bandaging in layers

New Kingdom period from the 16th to the 11th century BC

papyrus paper made from the pith of a reed plant

poultice dressing of bread, herbs etc. for a wound or sore

quarterstaff long, thick stick used for fighting

serf farmer who is not free to leave his village

shrine place where gods are worshipped

sickle sharp curved tool used for cutting wheat, reeds etc.

sidelock bunch of hair hanging from one side of the head

slave servant owned by his or her employer

tunic sleeveless knee-length garment, often pulled in at the waist

weaver person who uses a loom to turn yarn into cloth

wet nurse servant who feeds babies with her breast-milk

will written document listing who should get what from a dead person's property

Index

◄ ► ◄ ► ◄ ► ◄ ► ◄ ► ◄ ► ◄ ► ◄ ► ◄ ► ◄ ► ◄ ► ◄ ► ◄ ► ◄ ► ◄ ► ◄ ► ◄ ► ◄ ► ◄

Titles in the *Ancient Egyptian* series include:

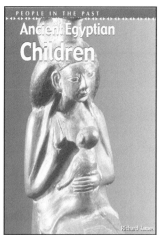

Hardback   0 431 14551 2

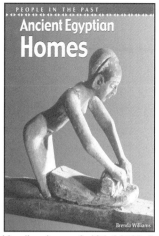

Hardback   0 431 14581 4

Hardback   0 431 14583 0

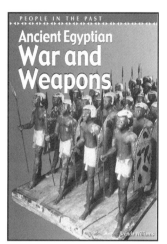

Hardback   0 431 14580 6

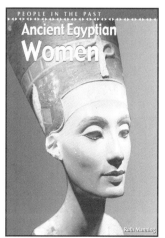

Hardback   0 431 14582 2

Find out about the other titles in this series on our website www.heinemann.co.uk/library